COLLEGE APPLICATIONS
Made Easy

Patty Marler ■ Jan Bailey Mattia

Printed on recyclable paper

VGM Career Horizons
a division of *NTC Publishing Group*
Lincolnwood, Illinois USA

Patty

For making me face my fear of outlines and for showing me the merit in opening a
book at the beginning, i am forever indebted.

Most of all,
for laughing, sharing and listening,
for your wisdom and your insight,
for your quiet strength of character,
and for believing and taking the risk…

thank you.

jan

Library of Congress Cataloging-in-Publication Data

Mattia, Jan Bailey.
    College applications made easy / Jan Bailey Mattia, Patty Marler.
        p.   cm.
    ISBN 0–8442–4344–2 (pbk. alk. paper)
        1. College applications—United States.   2. Universities and
        colleges—United States—Admission.   I. Marler, Patty.
    II. Title.
    LB2351.52.U6M28   1997
    378.1 0516—dc20   96–27779
                                                            CIP

Published by VGM Career Horizons, a division of NTC Publishing Group
4255 West Touhy Avenue
Lincolnwood (Chicago), Illinois 60646–1975, U.S.A.
© 1997 by NTC Publishing Group. All rights reserved.
No part of this book may be reproduced, stored in a retrieval
system, or transmitted in any form or by any means,
electronic, mechanical, photocopying, recording or otherwise,
without the prior permission of NTC Publishing Group.
Manufactured in the United States of America.

6 7 8 9 VP 9 8 7 6 5 4 3 2 1

Contents

CHAPTER 4: YOU WEREN'T ACCEPTED! NOW WHAT?   67

CHAPTER 5: CONSIDERATIONS FOR YOUR FUTURE   73

CONCLUSION   90

Introduction

So you've decided you want to go to college. Or, you've decided at the very least that you should take a serious look at it. Now what?! Though it seems like an education is essential for success in today's world of business, that doesn't help you decide which direction you need to go. There are thousands of schools and thousands of careers to choose from. Fear not! *College Applications Made Easy* will help you through the entire process, from how to decide what type of career is for you to what happens if you don't get accepted to the college of your choice.

"College is always on the road to somewhere else."

—Tom Robbins

Making Good Career Choices helps in the process of choosing the career that's right for you. Then you move on to *Finding the Best School*. *Pieces of the Application* outlines how to complete the various components of the college application. If you aren't accepted, then it's on to *You Weren't Accepted! Now What?* Finally, *Considerations for Your Future* looks at different aspects of college life.

Applying to college may sound like an overwhelming prospect at this point, but remember, the road to higher learning is an education in itself.

Special Features

Special elements throughout this book will help you pick out key points and apply your new knowledge.

 Notes clarify text with concise explanations.

 Helpful Hints make you stand out from the crowd of applicants.

 Job Jump Starts provide ideas to ease your transition from college to career.

 School Smarts suggest ways to make college life a positive and constructive experience.

 Money Talks gives you valuable tips on affording your education.

 Special Thoughts provide inspiration and motivation.

Get ready, get set ... you're college bound!

Chapter 1

Making Good Career Choices

Yay! Congratulations! Good for you! You've decided to go to college. You're taking a positive step toward your future by opening your heart and mind to new learning, new experiences, and new points of view. Your college education is an investment in the future—your future.

"Native ability without education is like a tree without fruit."

—Aristippus

With the decision to go to college already made, the only thing left to do is begin applying, right?

Sorry!

You're not quite ready yet. Choosing to *go* to college is only the first step in the process. You must now decide *what* you will study, and answer the proverbial "What do you want to be?" question. This question has been asked since you were playing airplanes as a toddler and there's no getting away from it, especially not now!

This question will be asked many more times in your life. Most people change careers at least five times in their lives so it is not uncommon to be 50 years old and still asking yourself "What do I want to be?"

Some people are lucky enough to have always known what they want to be. You may remember the classmate who in first grade was constantly checking your forehead for a fever, by fifth grade volunteered to draw a picture of the reproductive organs in sex education class, and in their final year of high school—after completing theirs, yours, and two other people's dissections—won the scholarship to attend a prominent medical college (which, of course, was their school of choice).

If this scenario describes you, then you have already made a career choice and you're that much closer to sending applications. If not, you have an important career decision to make.

Why Decide Now?

You may have thought about taking a few courses from a variety of programs to see what interests you. While this appears to be logical, you may want to rethink this.

Why?

- Shopping around for a career is very time-consuming. It will take years to "dabble" into each program, and you will accomplish very little.

 Education is expensive. Deciding what you want to do before you begin college will save money on tuition, books, and living expenses.

- You may not receive credit for all the courses you take, thus increasing how long it will take you to complete your formal education

Example

Ryley Jones wasn't sure of the direction she wanted to take with her education, but she liked statistics and thought she would check programs out through their statistics courses. In her first year she took statistics courses from the departments of psychology, sociology, and computer sciences. When she began her second year, she discovered she would only receive credit for one of the three courses. She was already half a semester behind in her education after only one year.

 Each program has its own course requirements and optional courses. These vary from program to program and from institution to institution. It is therefore important to know what you are specializing in before you decide which courses to take.

- If you haven't decided by now, you can't be sure you will decide by the time you are finished college. You may find yourself with a certificate in a field you aren't really interested in. Take concrete steps and choose a field of study now.

- The response to an employer's question "Why did you choose this career?" is much more impressive when you describe why you like it, rather than simply saying "Because I have the education for it."

 "Choose your rut carefully; you'll be in it for the next ten miles."

—Road sign in upstate New York

- You don't want to look back on your formal education as being a waste of time when it could have been a wonderful and exciting learning opportunity.

Career Decision-Making How To's

So how do you decide if you should be an ambulance driver, x-ray technician, or doctor? Do you approach Joe the butcher and ask what he thinks you would be good at? Or do you place all potential careers into a hat, close your eyes, and pull one out? Does the career assessment you completed in ninth grade have all the answers or does the college guidance counselor? Choosing a career can be a challenging process, but it does not have to be a painful one.

"Grant me the courage not to give up even though I think it is hopeless."

—Chester W. Nimitz

Dare To Dream

Too often we feel limited by what is considered by everyone else to be "best" for us, or by what others expect from us. We believe choosing a career is about finding a job that pays well and provides stability. While these things are important, we forget we actually have to do the work for 40 hours per week. A job that only provides security may pay the bills, but will you want to get up each morning?

"It's a funny thing about life; if you refuse to accept anything but the best, you very often get it."

—W. Somerset Maugham

Working in a field you are passionate about makes you feel vital, invigorated, and that what you are doing is important. You approach your job with enthusiasm and truly enjoy what you do. It is much easier to go to work each day feeling optimistic and involved than going in solely for the paycheck.

Consider...

If there were not restrictions placed on you—that is, you had enough money, enough time, could move whereever you wanted, had perfect grades, had no one else to consider and no responsibilities—what would you want to do? What would be your dream job?

Stop reading now and dream!

This is your dream job. Many people feel that dreams will and should remain dreams, and that the only reason they are dreams is because we can never achieve them. Don't let this pessimistic attitude grab a hold of you. Dreams are about what you want, those things your heart desires. Let your heart continue dreaming, and set your brain to attaining them.

"A dream is a wish your heart makes."

—Cinderella

How?

First, consider what, if anything, is stopping you from achieving your dream job.

A dream job may seem so wonderful that you may have a hard time imagining it can become reality!

If money, time, or grades are limiting you, then jump ahead to the section on *Grades, Money, and Time* and see what you can do to overcome these obstacles.

If there are other obstacles, seriously consider if they are valid reasons or if they are merely excuses. Write them down and look for ways to overcome them. Ask a friend or career counselor what they would do if faced with these hurdles. Work through all the valid reasons and forget the excuses.

You are that much closer to your dream job.

Buy a business card organizer and gather cards from everyone who may be able to help you with your job search when you graduate.

Next, begin thinking about your dream job not as a dream, but as a reality. See yourself actually doing this job. Remember, the things we desire most may seem unattainable simply because of our desire for them. Attaining a goal is often much easier than we think.

Take your dream job off its pedestal and look at it as reality. It will be much easier to achieve.

Interests and Likes

If no dream job came to mind, then begin thinking about the various activities or pastimes that interest you. It is important to enjoy what you do at work, so take a good look at your likes and dislikes.

What subjects did you like in school?

What activities did you enjoy as a child? As a teenager? As an adult?

Who do you admire? What is their occupation?

Which jobs seem interesting to you?

What are you especially good at?

Who you are and what interests you will help you decide what to take in college.

Ask yourself these questions and develop a list of things you like and are good at. These should help you to come up with career ideas. If not, take them to a professional career consultant who can suggest some alternatives.

Make a conscious effort to notice the various jobs people have. Keep your mind open to all alternatives.

Hobbies as Careers

Sometimes the things you really love are things you already do as hobbies. Maybe you love computers or enjoy fixing motors. Perhaps your recreational time spent fishing could translate into a career. Looking at the things you enjoy doing in your spare time may provide career ideas.

Caution!

When considering turning a hobby into a career, remember that what you now enjoy doing in your spare time will become a job. You will be doing it every day at work, so it may begin to lose some of its value and enjoyment as a hobby.

Take a day wandering around campus exploring buildings, libraries, and recreational facilities. You will discover many new things about your college.

Career Assessment Tools

Many schools, colleges, career planning organizations, and government agencies offer testing that may help you make a career decision. These testing or evaluative tools come in the form of career assessments, personality inventories, and aptitude tests.

"The longest journey is the journey inward."

—Dag Hammarskjold

Simply described, these tests look at your characteristics to develop a list of occupations to which you may be suited. When completing these assessments, you answer questions on one or a combination of the following areas:

- Your skills

- Your age

- Your interests

- Your past grades and education plans

- Your personality characteristics

- Your salary expectations

The theory behind these tests is that the answers you provide will generate a list of potential occupations or career choices that "fit" with who you are and what you want to be and do.

Review any assessments that were completed in the past. Aptitude tests and career assessments completed in school may be useful now.

So go out, take a test, and all your questions about choosing a career will be answered, right?

Wrong!

The people and companies who create the tests have their own beliefs and biases, and these will be reflected in the testing and its recommendations. Therefore, depending on who wrote the test, the career suggestions may or may not be consistent with your way of thinking. Also, different tests may provide different results, so it is to your advantage to complete more than one assessment.

These tests are a good place to begin and often provide useful information. They should not, however, be relied on as the ultimate decision maker.

The results will give you ideas on the kinds of jobs you may be interested in, but remember they are *only* ideas. Use these test results only as a guide, and do not make your final career decisions from them.

Career Counselors

High-school guidance counselors, college registrar consultants, and career practitioners are all excellent people to approach if you are having trouble making a career decision. They will help you to think about your goals and ambitions and help you come up with suitable career alternatives.

 A counselor's job is to help you discover the available options and narrow down the possibilities. He or she is not there to tell you which occupation to choose.

The main advantage to seeing a career counselor rather than simply completing a written test is that more of your personality characteristics can come through in a one-on-one meeting. The disadvantage is that these people are human and they may miss potential alternatives or suggest alternatives that may not be suitable for you. And, being human, they also have good and bad days.

If you have access to a career adviser or practitioner, make an appointment to take advantage of his or her expertise. Take the career assessments you have completed, as well as your own personal list of likes and dislikes. Speak honestly and openly about the career alternatives you have considered and ask for a professional opinion.

Be open to what career counselors have to say but do *not* expect a definitive answer to "What should I be?" At the most, expect a list of potential careers. This is for the best. It is ultimately *your* decision to choose the career for you.

Concerned Onlooker's Input

You may be amazed by how everybody and their dog seems to have an opinion on what you should do with your life. Your best friend thinks you would make a great mechanic, while your uncle feels you should go into computers. Your school counselor says you have the potential to obtain a degree and your neighbor says "Just get a job and forget that college stuff." And then there's the presence of the hardest-to-shake onlookers, your immediate family.

If your only reason for taking a particular program of study is because someone told you they would hire you, think again. Be sure you will enjoy an occupation before you jump into it.

Whose advice do you take?

The best answer, like the answer to *all* advice, is to take everything in, think about it, and if it doesn't feel right or jive with your way of thinking, then throw it out. Only take the advice and suggestions that seem right to you.

It's your education and your life, make the most of it.

While people may get upset if you don't follow through on their suggestions, think about how upset you will be if you don't like the occupation. Only *you* know what you want out of life (well, maybe you don't know yet) and you must be the final decision maker.

What's Available?

Careers you are unfamiliar with are options you are not giving a chance. With the advances in today's business world, new occupations and careers are continually arising and it can be hard to keep up with them. If you are making a career decision, it is important to be informed on what's available.

Example

Even when you *do* know about specific industries, you may be unaware of obscure positions available with them. The following are some vocations you may have never heard of or thought about:

Industry	Occupation
Production plants	Environmental technology
Computer industry	Computer assembly
Law enforcement	Internet monitors
Any big business	Workshop development
Any business	Training personnel
Oil and gas companies	Land agent
Publishing industry	Typesetting
Horse industry	Equine science
Working with the aging	Gerontology
Aviation	Aircraft skin repair
Heating and air conditioning	Air conditioning technology

If you didn't know a job existed, how would you have the opportunity to consider it?

Your local labor market information center will have information on new and obscure occupations. It is also a good idea to flip through various college calendars to see the variety of programs available.

Career specialists (particularly college and school counselors) have books that summarize programs offered by various institutions. They provide *general* information on programs, institutions, application deadlines, admission requirements, and so on. Ask to look at one of these, for you may learn about occupations you have never considered.

For current information on a program and related details, consult with college calendars. Do not rely on the summary books to provide exact details on their programs.

Make your career decision an informed one. Don't wait until after you have graduated from college to find out that there is a career that really interests you.

Grades, Money, and Time

Is it unrealistic for you to commit to a full-time, two-year program when you have three small children at home? Can you afford a top of the line college, where tuition is one-half of your yearly income? Are your grades good enough to get into the law school of your choice?

Whether you like it or not, grades, money, and time can be determining factors in the career and/or college you choose. It is important to remember, however, that if your heart is set on a particular career or college, then nothing should stop you. With a little creativity and a lot of hard work, *any* problem can be solved.

Depending on your circumstances, financial assistance for some college programs may be available through: Employment centers, disability plans, provincial state career services, government assistance programs, welfare services, and native affairs and workers' compensation programs.

Problem Solving

Grades. If your grades are not in line with your career aspirations, consider upgrading. Repeat courses to improve on your marks, or take the courses necessary to be accepted into a program. Hire a tutor to help you and work harder than you have ever worked before. If you truly want to improve, you will.

"The only thing that can stop any one of us from learning new behaviors is ourselves."

—Ernie Zelinski

Time. If it is difficult to commit to being a full-time college student, then register for part-time studies. There are also correspondence programs you can complete at home, which usually have more flexible time-lines. While these programs may take longer to complete than enrolling in a full-time program, they are better than not taking anything. By enrolling in one course at a time, you get that much closer to completing your education than if you took none at all.

 If you think two or four years is too long to commit to your education, consider where you will be in eight years without it.

Money. If you are wondering how you will pay for your education, seek out as many alternatives as possible. Look into scholarships, grants, loans, family assistance, and registered or subsidized education plans. Don't leave any stone unturned. Use your college-bound brain to come up with as many alternatives as you can think of.

 Most colleges and universities outline the scholarships and work-study opportunities they offer in their calendar or in a special awards publication.

Related Occupations

If you have a career in mind but feel that there are still obstacles blocking your way, don't give up yet. Look at related occupations that may be more realistic for you.

If you look for alternatives you may be amazed at the career options open to you.

Example

Doctor (post-doctorate degree) → Nurse (degree) → Nurse (Diploma) → Nursing assistant (certificate) → Porter (no formal education required)

Psychologist (post-doctorate degree) → Social worker (degree) → Social worker (diploma) → Group home assistant (certificate)

"Never, never, never, never give up."

—Winston Churchill

Engineer (degree) → Civil engineering technology (diploma) → Plant operator (certificate) → Product shipper (company courses and training)

Architect (degree) → Drafting (diploma) → Urban and regional planning (diploma) → Carpenter (trades certificate)

As you can see from these examples, if a specific career seems out of reach, there are always alternatives. Keep the doors open to careers you are interested in by exploring all options.

"Perseverance is a great element of success. If you only knock long enough and loud enough at the gate, you are sure to wake up somebody."

—Henry Wadsworth Longfellow

Now You Have an Idea

You've narrowed things down to several options but don't yet have a stand-out favorite. Do you begin the neighborhood survey again? Put it to a committee vote with your family?

Probably not.

Once you have a list of career options, it is time to begin considering them seriously. Many students have graduated from college only to find the work very different from what they thought it would be. Take steps *before* you begin college to determine if a field really interests you. Find out which occupations you are most likely to enjoy.

How?

Attend institution career days. Find out more about the programs you are interested in from students and instructors. Attend career days at different colleges and find out how their programs are similar and different.

 Attend workshops and seminars presented by people outside of the university. You will get a fresh perspective and meet valuable business contacts.

Speak with people who do the work. First hand information from people who actually *do* the work will tell you more than any college brochure. Ask:

- What is a typical work day like?

- What tasks are routinely completed?

- How much variety is there in the work?

- Is the work completed alone or with a team?

- Is shift work required?

- What are the working conditions like?
- What tasks are most enjoyable? Least enjoyable?
- Are there opportunities for advancement?

When calling to inquire about an occupation, ask if the person you are speaking with has the time to speak with you. If not, ask for a time when you can call back that is more convenient.

Most people are happy to share information about their jobs.

Conduct salary surveys. Find out how much money people in a specific line of work make.

- Contact companies and ask what the salary range is. Most human resource personnel will be more than willing to give you salary ranges for specific lines of work.
- Ask people who do the work what the salary range for their position is.

Ask for the salary "range" of a "position." People will be more likely to give you help you if you ask this way, rather than asking how much money *they* make!

- Visit your local labor market information center and find out what the salary prospects for the industry are. Most centers will have historical information on an occupation including salaries, number of people employed in the industry and type of employers. They often provide industry projections as well, so you may find information on what shape the industry will be in when you graduate from college.

Knowing what a typical salary is may help you decide if the career is for you.

Volunteer. An excellent way to gain first-hand knowledge about a career is by working in the field. The information you gain this way will be the most valuable when deciding if a career is really for you.

 Volunteering provides you with insight into an occupation, helps you get to know people in the field, and looks good on your résumé.

Job shadow. Ask an employee in the field if you can "job shadow" him or her for a day, following the person as they go about a regular workday. This will give you the perfect opportunity to discover what that job is like.

Research educational requirements. Contact colleges that offer programs in the field that interests you to find out about the educational requirements.

- Which programs are available?
- How long are the programs?
- What sort of a document will you receive—a certificate, diploma, or degree?
- What courses would you be required to take?
- What grade point average or SAT score is necessary to get into the program?

 Most of this information can be found in an institution's brochure or yearly schedule.

Know what you are getting into before you enroll in any program.

Are there any special requirements? Some programs have special requirements you may never have thought about. To become an electrician you need to have good color vision, whereas, to be a court reporter you need to have good hearing. Conduct some research to see if you meet all the requirements for a program.

What can you do when you graduate? Before committing to any program, find out what you can do with your education. Is your training so specific that you will be able to only have one type of job or is it so broad that you will have trouble convincing employers of its merit?

Example

Steve discovered that a number of different occupations interested him and realized he would probably change occupations numerous times during his career. He decided to obtain a political science degree, because he felt he could convince employers that every job had a political side. He knew it might be tough at times, but felt his degree would offer him the flexibility to try many different occupations.

Shawna, on the other hand, was interested in small engine repair. She discovered that, upon completing her education, she could work on small engines, but that larger engines would be out of her scope. Shawna knew that this was what she wanted to do and enrolled in the small engine repair course. She was very happy upon graduation.

Only you know how much of a challenge and change in routine you need to remain interested in your work. Determine if there are enough areas of expansion in the field to keep you challenged.

 Join associations related to your field. You will meet people who may become friends or business associates and who may put you in touch with prospective employers.

How long will your education be current? Your competitiveness in an industry depends on how knowledgeable you are. In some industries, like statistics, the theories and methods you learn at a university will probably be current for your entire career, while in other industries, such as Internet wizardry, what you learn may be outdated in six months.

You can remain current through practical experience, on-the-job training, and upgrading, but the amount of post-graduation education you will need varies from industry to industry.

While your education may remain current for a long time, this does not mean that you have nothing left to learn. New products, techniques, and procedures are always being developed. It is your responsibility to continue learning even after your college days are long gone.

If you enjoy change and look forward to continually upgrading your skills, then a fast-paced and rapidly changing industry may be the one for you. If you want most of your formal education to be complete after college, then it would be wise to choose a stable industry where your education will stay current for a long time.

Consult with program advisers and employers to find out how long your education will be up-to-date.

If you are planning to travel for a year after your education, consider completing your education at another time or taking a program that will be current for longer.

Whatever situation you find yourself in, it is important to remember that learning is a life-long process. You should always try to stay open to new ideas, courses, and methodologies.

Can you use your education elsewhere? If you should decide to change careers, can you use your education in another field?

Example

Education	Transferability to other occupations
Hearing aid practitioner	Limited—Program is skills-based and few other occupations require these skills.
Teachers aid	Some flexibility—May use skills in a variety of occupations dealing with children.
Business degree	Very transferable—May use the knowledge in almost any field by describing how your degree relates to the field.

 Any education is transferable to different occupations. The key lies in describing how your knowledge, skills, and ability to learn will benefit an employer.

Will you have to relocate to find a job? Job opportunities in some careers may require relocation.

Example

If you want to take an acting program, you should consider how much work you will secure if you live in Juno, Alaska. If you want to become the next Elizabeth Taylor, this may not be the best place to live.

If relocation is required, are you prepared to move? Are you ready to:

- Move away from friends and family?

- Have your spouse and/or children move to a new location?

- Live in a place you are not familiar with?

- Live where you have fewer support systems?

- Make new friends?

- Experience new cultures and ways of doing things?

- Take a challenge?

Your attitude can have a significant influence on how you handle moving. It is up to you whether it is a new and exciting adventure or a miserable challenge.

Research job opportunities in your area and others. If relocation is required, weigh this factor in before entering college. Your diploma in oil drilling is going to do you little good if you want to live in downtown Chicago.

Are the job prospects good? Will you have a job to apply for when you are done with school? This is a huge question, and clearly you want the answer to be "yes."

There is no way of knowing for sure what the future holds, but you can make educated predictions if you have the right information.

To find out what the job forecast for your occupation of choice is, consult with:

- Your local labor market information center
- Government employment centers
- Colleges that offer a program in the field
- Industries that hire people in this profession
- Employees currently working in the field
- Private career forecasting agencies
- Other surfers on the Internet

Begin reading the career section of the newspaper well before you begin applying for jobs. You will get an idea of what's available and have a better idea on what to apply for when you are done with school.

When you talk with others about the future potential in your chosen field, ask for their opinions of what the industry will look like when you graduate, in five years, and in ten years. Remember, you want to be employed for more than a few years—so find out the short range and long range forecasts.

 You're Getting Closer

Now that you have a good idea of what the programs you are interested in entail, it is time to make a decision. Choose the field that is going to meet your needs best *and* make you the happiest. A well-informed, thought out decision now will make your education and life after college much more fulfilling.

 "Self-trust is the first secret of success."

—Ralph Waldo Emerson

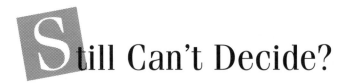 Still Can't Decide?

If you have completed the career searching process, still can't make a career decision, but are intent on going to college, then make sure you take a program that offers the most transferability and flexibility. If you aren't dead set on a particular career, it is good to choose a program that offers a wide variety of courses, so that when you decide what to specialize in, you will already have some of the required courses.

Example

After proceeding through the career decision-making process, Pat knew only that she wanted to take sciences in college and that she wanted to obtain her degree. She decided to choose a major by looking through the college calendar for the program that offered the most variability of courses. In her first year, she was a biochemistry major.

By the end of the second semester, Pat had taken a course that she was passionate about. Four years later, she graduated with a Bachelor of Science Degree with a major in Psychology.

 Even if you aren't clear on what you want to do, it still is possible to get the most out of your education and end up with a certificate you are happy with.

The Bottom Line

The bottom line is to enroll in a program you are interested in. If you *could* be a lawyer, *would* be a good mechanic, *should* go into the family business, your best bet is still to choose a career that makes you happy.

 "There is no sense in the struggle, but there is no choice but to struggle."

—Ernie Pyle

Chapter 2

Finding the Best School

Harvard. Yale. Stanford. Will one of those world-famous schools accept you? Do you want them to accept you? As important as deciding what to take is deciding where to take it. Choosing the institution that's right for you is a very personal decision. Shop around.

"Shoot for the moon. Even if you miss it you will land among the stars."

—Les Brown

Top 10 Reasons for Choosing a Specific College

1. You've heard there is great dating potential and you wouldn't want to miss finding your soulmate.

2. All your friends are going to that college, and you don't want to feel left out.

3. The picture on the front of the college brochure looks like the students are having a great time.

4. The temperature is warmer in Texas than in New York.

5. Your neighbor said their best friend's stepfather's cousin's son went to that college and thought it was great.

6. Mom and Dad already enrolled you.

7. The party-time to study-time ratio is 60% to 20% (with an extra 20% required for sleep.)

8. You don't know where else to go, so you might as well choose your local college.

9. You've seen several colleges' diplomas and CYT College uses the nicest paper.

10. Doctors Mr. and Mrs. Know It All obtained their degrees from XYZ school. If it's good enough for them, it's good enough for you.

Colleges, Colleges, Colleges

The education industry is a highly competitive one in which established institutions fight for students and new schools try to get in on the game. While this can be to your benefit, it can also work against you if you are not prepared for it. Make your college choice an informed one.

"In all human affairs there are efforts, and there are results, and the strength of the effort is the measure of the result."

—James Allen

Types of Colleges

Various types of colleges exist, each catering to students with varying academic backgrounds and educational needs. The institutions vary in their programming and their philosophies. Some of the various sorts of colleges are:

- Vocational/trade colleges
- Technical institutes
- Schools of nursing
- Academic colleges
- Universities

These institutions can be:

- Private
- Public
- Military

There are wide variations in accreditation, academic reputation, campus life, curriculum planning, and admission requirements. Because of this, it is important to research the school carefully and choose one that is the right match for you.

Some college campuses have on-site banks. They may offer special student rates, lower service charges, and student loans.

Educational institutions offer programs related to their purpose and mandate as an institution. While some colleges offer only degree programs, others have a combination of degree, diploma, certificate, apprentice, and continuing education programs. Still others have a curriculum designed for technical and trade programs. Different colleges specialize in different educational areas.

Post-secondary education reference books are available that summarize institutions and their programs. Contact a higher education career counselor to see one.

Take the time to find out which colleges offer the program you want to take. The institution you choose may impact the education you receive, so consider which school is right for you.

Read program descriptions carefully to determine if the focus and course material is consistent with the career you want.

Admission Requirements

Every program in every college will have specific entrance requirements. Whether you are applying to become a medical doctor or retail meat cutter, you must meet at least the minimum program entrance requirements.

Check with current college calendars for program admission requirements. Remember, every institution sets its own requirements, so look at each calendar.

The minimum requirements for entry will vary from program to program and from college to college. Most institutions use at least one of the following to determine eligibility:

- Grades from high school and post-secondary institutions

- Career investigation report

- Personal interview

- Related portfolio

- Résumé

- References

- Audition

For more information on the parts of the application, refer to Chapter 3.

If you are applying for a quota program (where only a certain number of students will be accepted into the program), you may have to do better than just meeting the minimum requirements. How institutions choose students will vary. Alternatives include:

- Accepting qualified applicants on a first-come, first-served basis

- Accepting only the *best* of all candidates

- Accepting those applicants who exceed the minimum qualifications by a predetermined amount

Once the quota is filled, no further applications are considered. If the program does not fill, students on a waiting list (who meet the minimum, but not the preferred requirements) will be accepted.

Ask if there is a program waiting list. Many students just like you are covering all their bases and applying to several different institutions. A student who is accepted at more than one college will leave an unfilled space at the colleges they do not attend. If you are on the waiting list at one of these colleges, you may still get in.

Consult with college calendars for exact admission requirements and deadlines.

 Apply well before the application deadline. Some institutions choose students based on a first-come, first-qualified basis.

College Program

Advancing your education and improving yourself is a positive step, but be wary of jumping into the first program that comes along. The program name may seem enticing, but if the courses can't be credited to your degree or don't interest you, then they will be a waste of time. Know about the program focus, what is required of you, and what documentation you will receive before making a commitment.

Read about:

- Admission requirements

- Required courses and their descriptions

- Optional courses and their descriptions

- Necessary volunteer experience

- Required practical experience

- Length of the program

- Special materials you must purchase

- Documentation you will receive upon completion

Knowing all you can about a program will help ensure that your education will be of value. Find out what you are getting into before making any decisions.

Special application considerations may be given to foreign, mature, and special students. Consult with the registrar's office to find out if you qualify for any distinctive treatment.

College Reputation

What is the college like? Do graduate students speak favorably about their education and life at college? Are well-respected instructors applying for tenure or does the college have a hard time finding good professors? Does the community feel the college is good, run-of-the-mill, or bad? Do employers prefer to hire graduates from other institutions? The answer to these sorts of questions can say a lot about the reputation of a college and its programs.

Many colleges use scholarships and other incentives to try to recruit students. Remember that education is a business. While college advocates and displays may make a college seem impressive, only your own critical evaluation can tell you if it really is.

Choose a school with a solid, good reputation. While college staff usually paint a beautiful picture of the college, be sure that professors, employers, students, other institutions, and the community look at it favorably as well.

Contact:

◗ Employers

◗ Graduates of the college

- ♦ Accreditation bureaus

- ♦ Local businesses

- ♦ Affiliated associations and organizations

- ♦ People working in the field

- ♦ The college Internet server

Ask as many people as possible their opinion of a college and its programs.

 If you are planning on obtaining a degree, consider attending a smaller college in your first year. You will receive more one-on-one instruction, meet more friends, and find the transition into college life easier.

Accreditation

Would you eat at a restaurant that did not meet health board standards for operation? Would you go swimming if maintenance and water standards were not met? If you would not do these things, then why would you attend a college that has not been accredited?

Accreditation associations monitor colleges to make sure they offer quality programming that will benefit students. While each region has its own accreditation standards and criterion, most schools are judged based on a combination of the following:

- The institution's goals and mission are soundly conceived

- The educational programs are intelligently devised

- The institution's purposes are being accomplished

- The community shows a need for the programs

- Qualified instructors and adequate staffing and organization are in place

- The institution merits confidence

Ask colleges about the accreditation they have received. It is in your best interest to attend an institution that offers quality training.

"I am the master of my fate; I am the captain of my soul."

—William Earnest Henley

Transferability of Credit

What if in five years you should decide to further your education—will the credit you receive now be transferred to other programs? To other colleges? While this may be the least of your worries now, it may make things easier later.

If a college's courses are transferable, it may be possible to take part of your program at one institution and complete it somewhere else.

Find out if the college you want to attend has agreements with other institutions to make the transferring of credit easy.

Remember:

How easy it is to transfer course credits may be related to the reputation of the college. Poorly respected colleges may have trouble making transfer agreements with other institutions, whereas highly respected colleges will not.

Instructors' Credentials

Where the professors were educated and how much education they have can say a lot about an institution. If the professors have impressive credentials from impressive institutions, there is a better chance that your education will be of a high standard. If on the other hand your instructors seem to meet the bare bones criterion, you would not be wrong to question the quality of education you will receive.

A college that is hesitant about answering your questions may be trying to hide something, or maybe not. Be persistent and give the college the benefit of the doubt. You may have just reached someone who didn't have the answers to your questions.

Graduation Documentation

Local College offers office administration as a *certificate* program, State College has a business *degree* program, and Next State College has a *diploma* program. So which one do you choose?

The type of documentation you receive at the end of your schooling will depend on the program you take.

- A *degree* is usually awarded after successfully completing a four-year, full-time program

- A *diploma* is awarded after completing a two-year, full-time program

- A *certificate* is granted after a program lasting several weeks to one year

- *Apprenticeships* are awarded after completing theoretical courses and a specified amount of time training on the job

- *Pre-technical* and *upgrading* programs provide you with the necessary knowledge to enter college programs.

The certification awarded often is dependent on the number of course hours/credits required to complete a program.

So why does it matter which document you receive?

Example

Sean at GTS Engineering was interviewing Alex Knewman for an electronics engineer assistant position. During the interview, Alex stated an interest in someday being promoted to head engineer of a project. After Sean stated that an Engineering *degree* was necessary for this position, Alex looked panicky and stated he thought he could do this with his education. Sean felt sorry for Alex when he began to explain the different job opportunities available to diploma graduates and degree graduates.

Find out what documentation you will receive upon graduation and most importantly, what job your education will qualify you for.

 Some employers and agencies may pay for an individual's training. If you are employed, consider asking your employer if they will sponsor your further education.

Job Placement Statistics

The curriculum and quality of education varies from college to college and employers often find that students educated at a particular institution are more qualified and prepared. If you find out that few employers hire people who have graduated from a specific institution, then you would be wise to choose another college.

Most colleges keep track of the employment status of their graduates, and will produce employment statistics. Research these to find out if graduates are getting jobs—*in their fields.* You want to attend a college whose graduates are in demand.

Develop good study habits early in your college career. Find a quiet place where you feel comfortable and develop a study schedule you can stick to. You will find yourself more prepared and less frantic when deadlines and exams approach.

Other Things to Consider

The quality of education you receive is critically important when choosing an institution, but there is more to a college than their academic credentials. The institution you choose should fulfill *all* your expectations, not just your academic ones.

Look into campus life before deciding on a college. Make informed decisions and your college experience is likely to be a positive one.

Cost

While it may not seem fair that you should have to consider cost when choosing a college, it is realistic. It is up to you to determine what you can afford.

Well known and respected colleges often cost more, but if you can't afford them you can still get quality education. Many affordable institutions offer good, reputable programs that are respected by employers, students, and other institutions.

Ask institutions about the financial assistance they offer to students. Each college has their own scholarships and financial aid packages, so check into them. Minimizing the cost of your education will ease the stress of going to school ... *and* the payments you have when you are done.

Scholarships and awards vary from institution to institution. Ask for a copy of each college's awards handbook.

Only you know how much you can afford to spend on your education. Draw up a detailed budget predicting the money you will need for tuition, books, supplies, and living expenses. Your calculations will be different for each institution, so complete a separate budget for each.

Institutions may "custom design" financial aid packages for students with special needs and considerations. Don't be afraid to ask.

Location

Where a school is located is another serious consideration. Many students want to go away to college; others prefer to stay at home. In making this decision, ask yourself the following:

- Can I afford to move away?
  The intrigue of living in a different city may be compelling, but is the added expense worth it?

- Is it necessary to move away?
  Can you get the education you want close to home or must you move away?

- How far away is far enough?
  Is moving to the next city far enough or do you feel you must move across the country? Before you decide, remember to consider what you can afford.

 Moving away is going to increase the cost of your education. When determining if you can afford it, consider everything from the college fees, to accommodation expenses, to telephone and transportation expenses.

- How important to you is it to have the support of family and friends? College will be an exciting time in your life, but it will also at times be trying. If you move away, the people you normally turn to will not be there. You must decide if this is something you can handle.

Just because all your friends are going away or staying home doesn't mean you need to, too. Do what's best for *you*.

Living Arrangements

Where will you live? Research the accommodation available at the colleges you are considering.

 Many colleges have accommodation registries to assist you with locating suitable housing.

At Home

Your first and probably least expensive alternative is to remain living at home. Living at home will mean you don't have the additional stress of locating affordable, safe and comfortable housing, your surroundings will be familiar so you won't have any new distractions, and you will have a support network right at your fingertips.

While you may be feeling the urge to move into accommodations of your own, this may not be the appropriate time for it. Moving out can be exciting, but it is also expensive and stressful.

Attending college and living at home can be a positive option.

College residences. Campus residences are designed for students to live in, but they vary in how appropriate they are for students. Some residences seem more like party buildings than living quarters, so it is important to look into them and consider how they will impact your education. Is your goal as a student to obtain the best grades possible or to drink the most beer?

"We are born to succeed, not fail."
—Henry David Thoreau

Look into how the accommodation is designed. Housing units vary from condo type living (where you live with two to five other students) to huge complexes (where several hundred students live in a single building). The type of building and layout of your dwelling may determine how easy it will be for you to study.

Possible Negative Aspects of Campus Residences

- Having to share bathroom and kitchen facilities. You may not know if you will have milk for your cereal if everyone uses the same fridge.

- The amount of quiet time. Many find that they have to study late at night or in campus libraries because quiet time in the dorm is almost non-existent.

- The amount of physical space. The motto "provide shelter for as many students as we can" often translates into itty bitty living space for each student. Can you handle this?

- Eating campus food. Often cooking facilities are not provided and students must eat at residence food service facilities. Meals may be no fuss but are they worth eating?

 Eating well can provide you with the energy and health you need as a student. This can be as easy as choosing a salad instead of a hamburger at a fast food restaurant. Get into the habit of eating healthy food.

- You never feel you leave the college. You may not get a break from campus life if you live on campus.

- The people. You don't get to choose who you live with so there is no guarantee you will like them.

- You have to move every summer. Some residences do not allow students to live on campus during summer breaks. This can be expensive, require a lot of effort and be a headache, especially if you are from out of town.

Possible Positive Aspects of Campus Residences

- Living with other students who understand the demands of college life.

- Easy access to classes, recreation facilities, libraries, health facilities, and more.

 Many housing units have residence coordinators who monitor students' concerns, mediate conflicts, organize special events and activities, and act as a liaison between college and students.

- Recreational coordinators who organize and promote activities for students.

- Food services, so you do not have to worry about food preparation.

- A greater chance of meeting people and developing friendships.

- A true sense of campus life.

 Living on campus will reduce the money and time you spend commuting.

A bad residence is something to be avoided, but a good residence can add a positive dimension to your life as a student. Check into them.

Private Residence

Living in a private residence alone or with roommates can be a great way to spend your college years—or it can be sheer terror. Before deciding to live in an apartment or house, be sure to consider:

- The expense. It will probably cost more to live in a private dwelling.

- How long it takes to commute. You will spend more time getting to and from college, time that could potentially be spent studying. Commuting time can, however, provide time to unwind, time you may not get if you live on campus.

 Review your class notes each day. You will remember what you learn better and reduce the time required to study at exam time.

- Your roommate(s). If you choose to live with a roommate, be sure you are compatible. Many best friends have turned into worst enemies after living together. Pick your roommate(s) carefully.

- If you can, live alone. You will probably get more studying done but if you don't like being alone this may not be your best choice.

- The availability of accommodation near the college. Housing close to college campuses is often in demand and may be hard to find. Look well in advance to be sure you are not scrambling to find a place to live.

Fraternities and Sororities

Living in these group houses usually requires an application for membership and acceptance into the "family." Fraternity and sorority houses often have specific ideas about behavior and etiquette and expect their members to act in accordance to their mandates. As a member, you would be living with a group of people who have certain philosophies and beliefs consistent with yours.

Choose accommodations best suited to you.

One can never consent to creep
when one feels an impulse to soar.

—Helen Keller

Part-time and Correspondence Studies

If you want to go to school only part time or wish to complete your studies at home through correspondence, you may have to find a college that can accommodate you. College policies vary and there may be special requirements or considerations for these types of studies. Take time to find out what they are.

Support Systems

Attending college can be stressful and it is important to have somewhere to turn. A good college knows this and provides resources to its students.

- Health services. Everyone gets sick sometimes, so easy access to medical treatment is essential.

 If you have special medical requirements, ask how the institution can accommodate you and what health services are available.

- Personal counseling. If you need to talk to someone about your personal life it is important to know that help is available. If you feel you will never need this service, remember that you never know what hand you will be dealt in life.

- Vocation counseling. What if you're no longer sure that the apprenticeship training you are taking is what you want? Should you continue on, should you drop out of school completely, or should you take something else? An academic advisor can help with decisions such as these. Be sure your college offers this service.

 In many smaller colleges the instructors and/or registrar may be responsible for counseling students academically. Don't be afraid to turn to them.

- Academic assistance. Who's going to help you when you don't understand what's going on in class? In high school, you probably would have turned to your teacher or a friend, but where do you go now? In small colleges, it may be like your old high school, but on large campuses, help often comes from teaching assistants or graduate students. Find out what sort of academic assistance (if any) is available to students.

- Job placement assistance. A college service that assists in job placement can be an asset. It is often a matter of getting your foot in the door, knowing which company has openings, or knowing who to contact which gets your career on its way. A college that helps its students find work is a college committed to helping students attain their career goals.

Don't wait until graduation to begin looking for work in your field. Take relevant summer jobs (even if they pay less than un-related work) and get to know employers in the field. Networking is the key to a successful job search. (For more information, you can refer to *Job Hunting Made Easy,* **by these same authors.)**

- Legal assistance. This, again, may be a service you feel you would never use, but you never know. Better to have it available than to have nowhere to turn if you need to.

- Pastoral care. Looking after yourself spiritually is important to your whole self. Find out what sort of pastoral services are provided and where they are located.

Attend a college orientation even if you are familiar with the buildings and layout. You may find out about things you never would have thought to ask about.

Campus Safety

What's the crime rate on campus? Are there security guards? How will you get from the library to your car in the lot at 11:00 at night? If the college doesn't have answers to these questions, are you going to feel comfortable? You want your focus to be on your studies, not on your safety.

If you are living alone, develop a safety buddy system with a friend. Check in with each other before you leave your apartment, after you get home, and at the end of each day. By doing this, if anything should happen to you, someone will be aware of it within hours.

Extracurricular Activities

Going to school doesn't mean you can't have fun, too. In fact, it is essential to your health and well-being to get involved in leisure activities (watching television does not qualify). Most colleges have recreational facilities, clubs, associations, and organizations for students. You know what type of activities you enjoy, so see if they're available on campus … and get involved in them.

While your first month at school may be hectic, now is the time to join in on extracurricular activities. It will be easier to meet people when everyone is new and you will develop a routine which includes time for yourself.

Intercollegiate Athletics

Go team go! College athletics may be a large part of your life, whether you are a spectator or participant.

If you plan on participating, ask:

- Do you have what it takes to make the team?
- How much of a time commitment is required?
- How much traveling will you be doing with the team?
- Are athletic scholarships available?
- How will your involvement affect your studies?

If you are an enthusiastic spectator, ask:

- Which sports are available at the college?
- Are admission fees less for students?
- Are the teams competitive?
- Does the college support and promote their teams?
- Are students encouraged to attend and cheer on their teams?

 "The world is moving so fast these days that the man who says it can't be done is generally interrupted by someone doing it."

—Harry Emerson Fosdick

Extras

Each person has their own feelings about what makes a good college. Consider the things that are important in your life and see how a college measures up to your needs. Other things to consider may be:

- Campus food services
- Discrimination and harassment policies

- Equal opportunity practices

- College philosophies and mission statements

The more information you gather about a college, the better prepared you will be. Leave surprises for your birthday parties—not for your education.

Chapter 3

Pieces of the Application

"Above all, try something."

—Franklin D. Roosevelt

Much of what is asked on the college application form is fairly standard in the United States and Canada. There are a few differences and a few extras some schools throw in, but there is a reason for everything.

Every college needs certain information simply to enter you into the computer system, give you a file or student identification number, and keep you registered as an individual in a specific program.

This information includes:

- legal name

- date of birth

- country of citizenship

- current address and phone number

- Social Security or Social Insurance number

- Primary, or first, language

- Emergency contact numbers

Then, of course, there is education-specific information required by the college or university. This is more specific information which can dictate if you qualify for enrollment at a particular college. For example:

- Whether you have applied to the institution before

- Your educational background

- Whether you are presently attending other post-secondary schools

- Whether you have official transcripts of marks from all other schools you have attended

- Which program are you applying to

Be sure to include all information asked for by the college. If something is missing, your application will be delayed, or you may simply receive a rejection letter in the mail.

Additionally, you will often be asked to provide some information voluntarily. Such information can be considered optional, and is often listed as such on the application form. This information is often used for statistical purposes to indicate the kind of people applying for post-secondary education. The type of questions asked may include:

- your gender

- your marital status

- your ethnic background

- whether or not you have a disability or handicap

- whether you plan to seek employment while in school

- if you are employed, how many hours per week

Again, this information is voluntary and should you choose not to answer, it will not affect your application.

These are the standard questions you may expect to answer on most application forms and if they were *all* you had to expect, college applications would be completely painless! Unfortunately, most colleges and universities add a few extra questions to their applications to assist them in determining what kind of students are best suited for, and would benefit most from, their programs.

Pay attention to deadlines for applications. The sooner you get all the correct pieces of your application package in, the better.

Investigating Careers

In Canada, many schools require applicants to submit a Career Investigation Report (CIR). Although they are not required of students in the United States, these reports offer a terrific opportunity to find out more about a career field before investing in years of education. Whether or not you prepare a CIR, a little career research now will pay off in the future.

An effective career research effort should provide you with answers to the following questions:

- What are the job possibilities in this field?
- Is the industry expanding?
- Will I have to relocate to find work?
- How much money can I expect to make?
- What are the educational requirements for success?
- What is a typical workday like in this field?
- Is there opportunity for advancement?

Need a little more to go on? Here's all the information you'll need to get started with your career investigation:

"It takes time to be a success, but time is all it takes."

—Anonymous

Where Do I Start?

Assuming you know very little about the industry and program you are applying to, the easiest and most comfortable place to begin is with the school itself.

1. Read through the literature in the school calendar.

2. Chat with a counselor about the program and types of career it caters to.

3. Ask to speak with students currently enrolled in the program.

4. If possible, speak to a graduate of the program working in the field.

Once you have exhausted those information sources, pick up the phone and explore some more options.

Who Do I Call?

Who are you comfortable calling? Start with these people.

1. Friends or acquaintances who are in the industry.

2. Anyone they know in the industry or a related industry.

Don't know anyone?

3. Pick up the phone book and call businesses that would use your services after you completed your education.

4. Ask new people you meet in business and in social situations what they do. You may be surprised who can offer you information, contacts, ideas, or suggestions.

 Make your phone calls first thing in the morning before people are too wrapped up in the business of the day to talk with you.

What Do I Ask?

Certainly what you ask will depend on how much you know going into the conversation. Additionally, you must determine what is important to you in a career or a working environment. Those things should certainly be on your list to ask.

- What is the salary range for this type of position?

- Is there the opportunity for travel?

- Will I have to consider relocating to another town, state, or province?

- Is there room for advancement in your company or in the industry?

- Is it essential that I sit at a desk all day?

- I enjoy interaction with people. Is that something I can expect in this type of career?

- How would you describe a typical day?

- What would you say are the best and worst parts of your job?

- How much room is there for creativity in your career?

- Is there any physical labor required to be successful in the position?

- How flexible is the work environment?

Have a list of questions written down and in front of you. You want to be and sound prepared, and you don't want to have to call back later saying, "I forgot to ask ...".

In addition to the concrete questions you can ask about work environment, prospects for the future and salary expectations, it is essential you determine for yourself if you are realistically suited to this occupation. Be sure to ask:

- Beyond what I learn in school, what characteristics, skills, and/or attributes are necessary to succeed in this field?

  The answer to this question may be the most influential because:

  You may discover ... that keen attention to detail is essential, but even the thought of that bores you to tears!

  You may discover ... you must be able to type at least 85 words per minute, and the arthritis in your fingers makes that physically impossible.

  You may discover ... your first few years will be spent in the mail room—no matter what your education is.

You may discover … no matter what, two weeks of every month will be spent traveling—and flying terrifies you.

These may be the types of things that help you determine whether or not this is the career for you. Remember, you career choice will probably last at least five years. Are all the elements there to make it an enjoyable and productive time?

Why Would They Talk to Me?

Right off the top, when you reach someone on the phone, introduce yourself and explain why you are calling. People are often more receptive when they know you aren't calling to try and take their job or sell them something they don't want!

Try:

"Hi, my name is Chris Davey. Pat Jones suggested I call. I'm applying to the computer systems program the the Tech Institute and was wondering if you could spare a few minutes to chat with me about your job.

 It's a good idea to jot down a bit of a script before you make your first call. You may be nervous and it will help you sound prepared.

You will probably be surprised at how willing people are to talk to you about their career, particularly if they enjoy their job! Provided you don't take up a lot of their time and are prepared with specific questions, you will no doubt get the information you are seeking.

 If you do come across someone unwilling to chat with you, don't be discouraged. Maybe they had a bad day or are under a tight deadline. Ask if there is a better time to call. If not, call someone else.

Where Can I Find More Information?

Depending, of course, on the particular career you are investigating, there are ways other than speaking with people directly involved in the industry to gather information.

What?

1. As a good general source, try the library. Public libraries often have a variety of career reference books. Depending on the library, you may be able to find considerable information. Certainly, the more obscure the career you are looking for, the less likely it will be in the library, but it is a good place to start.

 For some additional ideas about how to network, please see *Job Hunting Made Easy*.

2. Many cities have government sponsored specialized libraries called labor market information centers (or something similar). These are libraries designed specially for career information. There you can find information about everything from salary ranges for a particular career, to information about how many new employees were hired in the past year, to what percentage of workers in the industry are female versus male, and so on. Again, you will find some careers are easier to investigate than others.

3. Another source that may be very helpful to you are government employment centers. Sometimes these are private companies funded by the government and sometimes they are listed under government services. Wherever they're listed, employment centers can be helpful in giving you an idea of the availability of jobs in the field you are interested in.

 While you're at the employment center, take a look at the job posting board, or through the job listings computer at what type of industry has need for employees. There's no point getting an education in a field with no job prospects.

4. It is a great idea to regularly scan the career section of your local paper, or better yet, papers from a number of cities. Are there regularly jobs advertised in the career you are interested in? Are there ever careers advertised in the field you want to study?

 Keep records of the people with whom you speak. These same people may help you when you finish school and begin looking for work.

 "One doesn't discover new lands without consenting to lose sight of the shore for a very long time."
—Andre Gide

Now that you have a better sense of where you want to end up, you'll be able to get the most out of the time you spend in college.

But wait! You still have to complete the application! There are a number of parts to every college application. We'll begin with the personal statement.

 ersonal Statements

The personal statement is your chance to outline for the admissions committee the qualities and characteristics that make you well-suited for the career and program you have chosen. Unlike the Career Investigation Report, the personal statement is often used for graduate programs, where the number of applicants accepted into programs is smaller. With this in mind, admissions committee members like to know a little more about each applicant as an individual—from what they do with their spare time to how they would contribute to the faculty and the profession as a student and as an individual. This is your time to talk about you as a person and what distinguishes you as an applicant.

There are a variety of things you may wish to include in your personal statement:

What?

1. Your choice of undergraduate studies and institution.

    There are occasions when your undergraduate degree may not be directly related to the graduate studies you are pursuing. For example, you may be applying to the Faculty of Law and your undergraduate degree may be in chemistry. You may wish to outline in your personal statement why you chose a particular undergraduate degree and how that degree benefited you and/or will benefit you in your graduate studies. Basically, how have your undergraduate studies prepared you for the graduate program you are applying to?

 "The biggest things are always the easiest to do because there is no competition."

—William Van Horne

    You may also wish to include why you chose the college or university you did for your undergraduate degree, especially if it is a prestigious one or one well known for preparing students for a specific career. If you chose the school simply because it was the same one your girlfriend was going to, you should probably leave that part out!

2. Any irregularities in your education or academic record.

    This is your chance to explain why you started late at a university, took a year off in the middle, had to withdraw from a class, or received an unusually low grade in a particular class. These are the type of things that can reflect badly on your standing as an applicant. Grade point average requirements are creeping higher and higher for college applicants so if there is a valid reason why yours is not as high as it could be … explain it!

Remember to simply explain your situation and the reasons for it. *Don't apologize.* Look for positives and highlight them.

3. Your non-academic accomplishments.

   This is a very important component of the personal statement. This is your chance to discuss all the "extras" that don't really have a place on the application form.

What?

Do you volunteer? Talk about the volunteer work you do that is directly related to your chosen field, has prepared you to work with all sorts of people, or has helped to develop you as an individual.

What do you do in your spare time? Discuss the extracurricular activities you are involved in and how they have contributed to your development as an individual. Participating in everything from sports teams to the student newspaper teaches you skills you will use in virtually every career. It is up to you to show the admissions committee how your activities fit in to the overall picture of what you will do in college.

 Take advantage of the personal statement. You may not have another opportunity to sell yourself.

Have you worked in the field? Be certain to give examples of any part-time, term, or contract work you have done that is related to the program you are applying to. This shows the admissions committee you are serious about your career choice, you have taken the initiative to work in the field already, and you are obviously aware of what is necessary for you to be successful.

4. Any circumstances that have or will contribute to your academic success.

This information may include anything from:

… you are lucky enough to have a full scholarship so you won't have to work during school. You will, therefore, be able to devote full-time attention to your studies.

to

… your parents are partners in a law firm they would like to retire from when you receive your law degree.

to

… you have worked part-time at Widget Incorporated for the last four years and they have guaranteed you a full-time position as soon as you graduate.

Whatever you feel will benefit you and your studies, mention it! You never know what may spark the interest of the Admissions Committee reviewing your application.

 It is not necessary to include research you have done with respect to the program you wish to enter. Take this time to talk about *you.*

Example

Attention: Admissions Committee, Department of Physical Therapy

"Education is not the filling of a pail, but the lighting of a fire."
William Butler Yeats

My goal, since grade 10, has been to become a physiotherapist. Since that time I have worked hard to learn as much about the industry as possible, including volunteering my time to get a head start on my education. I volunteer as a physiotherapist's aide on weekends and during the week. In my spare time, I volunteer at the seniors' center coordinating activities for the residents. I have gained considerable knowledge and insight into the needs of seniors and, as a result, have decided to specialize my practice when I graduate.

continued

As indicated on my transcripts, between the second and third year of my undergraduate degree (my major was psychology), I took a year's leave of absence to travel to Australia, New Zealand, and Asia. This was an exciting, challenging, and invaluable experience that assisted my education in ways I never expected. I have a greater appreciation for other cultures and definitely for other forms of medicine and treatment of ailments.

My undergraduate psychology degree has provided a sound basis for the further education my career choice requires. My writing skills are strong and my communication skills are excellent. Most importantly, I genuinely enjoy the volunteer and part time work I do and know I have chosen a career path I will be successful in and enjoy. I look forward to taking the first step toward that career with your school.

Sincerely,

Bret Cartier

As a final note, there is usually no stipulation regarding the length of your personal statement. Be sure to include all relevant information, but also be sure to make it interesting. It won't do you any good to discuss all the attributes that will make you successful at a university when it's too boring for anyone to read all the way through it!

Example

Personal Statement of Graham Chandry:
Theology Masters Degree Program

Excellent communication skills, compassionate and caring, strong convictions, and a life dedicated to God are a few of the qualities which make me an excellent candidate for the theology Master's Degree Program. A dedicated student and missionary, I believe that there is no better course of study for me and no more eager and determined student than myself.

I began my Christian journey as a teenager when my friends were attending a Christian rock concert. Not wanting to feel left out, I began attending church. Little did I know that within six years I would become a regular churchgoer, a choir member, committee organizer, Bible study coordinator, and missionary. My passion for theology peaked even more when I attended the

continued

University of British Columbia and discovered that I had only touched the tip of the iceberg.

After receiving my bachelor's degree, I took a year to contemplate the direction I would take in my life. After serious personal introspection and consultation with my family and church family I feel obtaining a master's degree is the best course I could take.

My thirst for theological growth is great and if accepted into the Master's Degree Program, I would use this opportunity to become a better and stronger individual, and then help others to do the same.

Sincerely,

Graham Chandry

Statement of Intent

Perhaps even more similar to the Career Investigation Report than the personal statement, the statement of intent outlines for the admissions committee what you intend to do with your education.

This is your opportunity to outline:

• your goals for the future

• where you see yourself in the industry you have chosen to pursue

• how you will contribute to that industry

• how you will contribute to the school along the way

It is beneficial for a school to have graduate students who go on to be successful in their field of study. Why? It looks good for them from a funding perspective—if they are able to list successful people who have graduated from their institution, private and public funders are more likely to agree the school does a good job and should continue to be supported.

If you present yourself as the determined individual you are, with clear goals and your path to success mapped out, the admissions committee is likely to see you as someone who can benefit the school while you benefit yourself.

This is where your knowledge of the career and industry you have chosen will pay off. It is much easier to define your goals when you know how an industry "works."

So what's left in this seemingly endless process? Well, there is the possibility of a few things … Honest, just a few!

English Competency Exam

Because there are many students attending universities and colleges who come from other countries, and because in recent years there have been cases of university-level students with grade-school English skills, many schools have implemented English competency exams.

The purpose of these exams is simply to assess a student's written English. It is a straightforward test, in which you must compose a standard essay usually on one of three topics provided by the examiner. You are passed or failed on the basis of sentence structure, spelling, and grammar—*not* content (in other words, your opinions are not graded). If your grammar is poor, your sentence structure inadequate, or you have more than a specified number of spelling mistakes, you fail.

 Keep your essay simple. Remember, you have limited time, and you are not being graded for your fascinating and complex ideas on the subject.

If you do not pass, the exam does not necessarily disqualify you from attending college. It usually means, however, you will have to take a remedial English course along with your other first semester courses, so that you can improve your writing skills.

Remember, the university or college you are applying to may use different names for these various application requirements.

TOEFL/TWE (Test of English as a Foreign Language/Test of Written English)

Both the TOEFL and the TWE are designed specifically for students whose first language is not English. The application form will ask what your primary language is and—if it is not English—if you have taken these exams. These are standardized tests offered at specific times throughout the year through the Educational Testing Service in your area and are required of all foreign students.

Other English competency tests include: COPE Test (certificate of proficiency in English), Michigan English Language Testing System, and the International English Language Testing System.

You will be asked to have the results of your TOEFL or TWE sent directly from the Educational Testing Service to the university or college to which you are applying. This is an important part of your application; be sure to complete it promptly so your application may be considered.

Specialty or Standardized Exams

Some programs, though not all, require applicants to take a standard-ized test and submit these scores with their applications. These stan-dardized test (meaning standard throughout Canada and the United States) scores are used in conjunction with your grade point average and other application components to determine your probability of success in your studies.

"You can lead a man up to the university, but you can't make him think."

—Finley Peter

The tests are developed by agencies other than the university you are applying to, and may not even measure knowledge specifically relat-ed to the field you wish to study. Strange? Yes, we would agree.

Tests such as the:

GMAT—Graduate Management Admission Test

GRE—Graduate Record Examination

MAT—Miller Analogies Test

LSAT—Law School Admission Test

and so on primarily test your ability to take tests.

Years ago universities found a correlation that suggested people who did well on these types of tests also did well at a university. As a result, some graduate schools insist on students taking these standardized exams. If your marks are competitive enough to get you admitted, but your LSAT score, for example, is not very high, consider taking the exam again. That is how heavily some schools rely on the test scores!!

You can buy books specifically written to help you prepare for these tests. We suggest you invest in one. Choose one that is regularly revised to keep up with changes in the exam.

Personal Interviews

Personal interviews for school are very similar to personal interviews for employment. They are often used where the admissions committee wants to get an impression of the individuals applying for the program. This is the time for you to convince the committee of your interest in the program, your knowledge of the career, and your goals for the future. Again, treat it as you would an interview for employment—sell yourself, your skills, and any relevant experience you have that would help you succeed in your studies.

You may be interviewed by one or more people as an individual or in a group setting.

Auditions

Auditions are reserved for fine arts programs at colleges and universities. If you wish to attend any program for music or theatrical arts, be prepared to have to audition for your place in the program. This is something you will be called upon to do if your application passes the preliminary screening stages. The school will notify you when auditions will be held. Be certain to prepare as you would for any competition or audition for a substantial role. Remember you only have one shot at it—give it your all!

"Courage is doing what you're afraid to do. There can be no courage unless you're scared."

—Eddie Rickenbacker

Portfolios

Portfolios may be submitted with your application or they may be viewed at a personal interview with the admissions committee. If you are applying to a photography program, or any type of fine art program, be prepared to show your portfolio, no matter how extensive it is. Make a point of presenting your best drawings, photographs, or pictures of your paintings or sculptures in a professional manner. Have them neatly displayed in a professional looking portfolio and be prepared to answer questions regarding your work.

Granted, it is sometimes difficult to show your personal portfolio to people, particularly those who are there to evaluate it. If you don't normally show your work to others, start. It will be good practice for you when you must show it to the admissions committee. Above all else, be proud of what you have done, no matter the outcome of your meeting!

Résumés

Yes, résumés! Some programs do ask that you submit a résumé with your application. Why? Similar to the personal statement, a résumé shows the admissions committee what you have done with yourself prior to applying to their program. Have you done any work related to the education you are interested in? Have you volunteered your time in a relevant area? These types of things can show the committee how motivated you are and how prepared you are for your education and for the career search that will follow it.

References

A reference for college is used in the same way references are for employment. Usually they are from past professors who can recommend your work to the graduate studies admissions committee, or they are from people working in the business you are wanting to study. Again, this is simply a type of confirmation or guarantee for the faculty you are applying to that you are capable, willing, and interested in succeeding in your studies.

 As you go along in your school and work career, it is a good idea to get reference letters from appropriate people along the way. You never know when they may come in handy.

Application Checklist

You're done—and you lived through it! Before you put all your hard work and time-consuming effort into an envelope and mail it away to the schools of your choice, read through the checklist … just to be sure.

- Did you complete everything on the application form?

- Is it neat and easy to read?

- Did you complete and enclose all additional information requested?

  – personal statement

  – statement of intent

  – other supporting materials (as requested)

- Have you arranged for the Educational Testing Center to forward your TOEFL/TWE marks to the school?

- Have you enclosed official transcripts of your marks or notarized copies (whichever the school requests)?

- Once again, did you complete everything on the application form?

Remember, every component of the application package has a purpose, and must be completed for the school to assess your application. Take the time to ensure everything is complete and enclosed. If you are missing a component of the package your application may be returned to you, or you may simply receive a rejection letter.

 Some schools do not accept applications directly. You may send all relevant information to an application center with your top three school choices listed. The application center then processes your application and decides which school you will be accepted to.

Chapter 4

You Weren't Accepted! Now What?

That awful form letter arrived in the mail with the bad news, "We regret to inform you …" Take a day to rant and rave, sulk and ask "Why me?"—but after that it's back to work. Don't throw in the towel yet.

"Turn your stumbling blocks into stepping stones."

—Anonymous

This is only *one* rejection letter, and if you've kept your options open, there are still several institutions left to contact you. See what they have to say before you begin to panic.

Should the worst scenario happen, and all the colleges you applied to send rejection letters, then it's time to make some serious career decisions. The *hard* work begins now.

Where Do You Go From Here?

First, find out *why* you were not accepted. You can only improve on your application if you know where the weak spots are. Then it's on to more self-evaluation, planning, and preparation. You will really begin to sweat now.

"We have a problem. 'Congratulations.' But it's a tough
problem. 'Then double
congratulations.'"

—W. Clement Stone

Get answers to these questions so you know what to improve on:

- Why your application was denied?

- What program eligibility criterion did you not meet?

- Were your grades too low?

- Were there questions left unanswered in your career investigation report?

- Did you apply too late?

- Were you next in line or the last person they considered?

- Are you on a waiting list or is there one you can get on?

- Is there anything you can do to improve your chance of being accepted next time?

Answers to these questions may be found in the letter you received, or you may have to contact the college registrar's office. Be sure you clearly understand the reasons why you were not accepted. Keep asking until all your questions are answered.

This is only a *temporary* setback.
When you consider how long you
will be working in your career, waiting another six months or a year to
try again is not much time at all.

Should You Appeal?

If you feel the reasons that you were not accepted are not good enough, you may consider appealing. Prepare sound arguments as to why you feel your application was not given adequate consideration.

Take an objective look at the application package you submitted. Does it adequately portray your skills, desire, and knowledge for a program? Is it *really* the best you could do?

Before you appeal, ask yourself:

- Are the reasons for rejecting my application valid?

- While I may be a great candidate for the program, did my application package portray this?

- If I had been on the selection committee, would I have chosen my application as one of the ones to be accepted?

If you still feel that your application warrants being admitted to the program, then proceed with your appeal. Contact the college and ask about their appeal process. Complete the required appeal forms, prepare your arguments, and convince them that your application should have been given further consideration.

Being one of the most suitable people for a program does not necessarily mean you will get in. It is your application package that is used to evaluate your suitability, so it must be completed well.

Is Your Career Choice A Good One?

You have already decided on the career for you, but this may be the time to take another look at all your options. While you may really think obtaining your degree and becoming a dentist would be great, are your grades more consistent with becoming a dental assistant?

Review Chapter 1: *Making Good Career Choices* to help you decide if the career choice is still a good one. Maybe other fields you were interested in seem more in line now. If not, then continue to go for your original choice!

Apply Again

Do it again, but this time do it different ... do it better. Make your application package so impressive that next time there is no way you can be turned down.

"If at first you don't succeed,
try, try again."

—William Edward Hickson

How?

- Find out what the people who *were* accepted put in their application package.

  The more information you have about what makes a good application package, the better. You can use other people's ideas and suggestions to make your package a better one.

- Do more research on your career choice and rewrite your career investigation report or statement of intent.

  Change, revise, edit, redo. Spend more time thinking, organizing and writing, and include everything you know about an occupation (even things you last time thought may be insignificant). The more thorough you are, the more your knowledge and enthusiasm will come through. A complete, well-written, and highly organized report will not go unnoticed.

- Find a related job.

  For the next six months or a year, work at a related job. If you want to become an X-ray technician, take a job as a hospital orderly. If you are considering a computer repair program, find a job in a computer store. These related jobs will provide you with more knowledge about your career of choice, give you valuable experience, *and* pay the bills. It will also look impressive on your application.

"Opportunity is missed by most people because it is dressed in overalls and looks like work."

—Thomas A. Edison

- If you cannot find a paying related job, volunteer. Demonstrate your enthusiasm and interest by working for the love of it.
- Take upgrading courses.

  Improve your grades and you improve your chance of getting into college. Find out which course grades had the most impact on your being rejected from the college and improve on these.

Taking upgrading courses will improve your marks and get you back into the swing of being in school.

- Practice your interview skills.

  If a personal interview was required, fine tune your presentation skills. The difference between being accepted or not may be in *how* you present what you know.

- Apply earlier.

  Next time, apply *early*—not on time. Quota programs that select students on a first-qualified, first-selected basis may be filled even before the application deadline arrives. Get your application in early.

- Apply to more colleges.

  If you feel you are a good candidate for a field of study, then there is probably an institution that agrees with you. Apply to several different colleges. Keep as many doors open as possible.

What you do now can make a difference next time you apply. Make a commitment to yourself to do all that is possible to get into college ... and you will.

 "I would never have amounted to anything were it not for adversity. I was forced to come up the hard way."

—J.C. Penney

And most importantly, *don't* give up on your dream.

Chapter 5

Considerations for Your Future

"The world stands aside to let anyone pass who knows where he or she is going.

—David Starr Jordan

Perhaps one of the more challenging things to stay focused on while you're going to a university is, believe it or not, the future. Colleges and universities have a strange way of consuming your life, because they are a world unto themselves. You go to classes and study every day, your friends are all there, you hang out at campus facilities, you go to parties there, you may even live on campus, so it's easy to forget that an outside business world exists. School becomes your way of life. Unfortunately, if you allow yourself to become *completely* consumed by campus life, it will make it all the more difficult to find employment after graduation.

So how do you combat this sneaky enemy? Always keep the word "job" in the back of your mind. How will this, what I am currently doing, help me find employment after graduation? Of course, you have to be involved in things happening on campus, but be sure you are aware of what is happening around you in the business community. Don't lose sight of your end goal, a career.

The road to higher education and a new career takes a lot of work. Don't forget to have fun once in a while. It will make you more productive.

he Work Habit

Obviously, the best way to keep in touch with the "outside" world while you go to school is employment.

1. If you work to put yourself through school, try and gain employment related to your overall career goal—no matter how remotely.

   So you want to be in advertising and the only job you can get for the summer is a "fun facilitator" at a summer camp for kids. Well, design a brochure to advertise what activities are available for the kids. Organize an activity where the kids get together and create their own television commercials, which you videotape for viewing.

   Be creative, you may be surprised at the connections you can make between where you want to be and where you are now!

 If you need to apply for financial aid, make it one of the first things you do. You don't want to find yourself ready to register with no money to pay for your courses.

2. If you are unable to find related employment, try, in whatever you do, to progress and diversify. The more experiences you can offer a potential employer the better.

   So you plan to waiter because the money you can earn is hard to beat, but you can't really see the connection between the restaurant business and your chemistry degree. Well, no matter what career path you choose, you will no doubt have to work with people, be they clients, your boss, or a customer.

   There is no better way to learn to interact well with people than as a waiter. You will also learn to prioritize your time like never before, and pick up transferable skills. You get the picture?

Loans for students are often a fact of education. Student loans are often offered at a lower interest rate and normally repayment doesn't begin until after graduation.

3. If you are fortunate enough to not have to work your way through college, volunteer.

    Granted, it would be a whole lot more fun to spend your spare time skiing or hanging out in student lounges, but that kind of experience doesn't translate well onto a résumé. Volunteer at least a portion of your time in a field you are interested in—it will help round out your résumé and it will probably make you feel great in the meantime.

    It does seem like a rather dull existence, living your life according to what can expand your résumé, but, unfortunately, until you are established in a field it is an important consideration.

Talk to people in the field you hope to enter. What types of part-time work did they do? What helped them the most? What would they do differently?

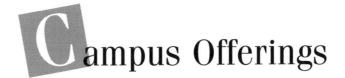

Campus Offerings

Even if you decide not to work while going to school, there are a number of things you can become involved with on campus to enhance your experience and build your résumé.

Student Unions

One of the benefits of going to school on a larger campus is that they are often run like mini-cities with many similar operating systems. Universities, colleges, and technical schools all have student unions, for example, which operate similarly to any political organization or bureaucracy. Having student union experience on your résumé can be quite impressive if you wish to pursue a career in politics, government administration of any kind, or business—where you must deal with board members. More importantly, joining one of these organizations while you are still in school affords you the opportunity to be a part of the workings of a political/bureaucratic type system and decide if it really is the niche you want to be involved in.

Regardless of the type of career you wish to pursue, Student Union experience demands excellent organizational skills, communication skills, and team work. It also teaches you the meaning of dedication and hard work! These are attributes which are impressive on any résumé.

Often we find ourselves basing our career aspirations on a somewhat misguided notion of what that career entails. Better to get involved now and find out than after you have your Economics degree!

"The future is not a gift—it is
an achievement."

—Harry Lauder

Special Interest Groups

A special interest group is basically just what it sounds like: a group of people, bound together by a similar interest, who get together on a regular basis to discuss or actively pursue that interest. The organization you choose may advocate for political change, fundraise for a particular cause, lobby government for change, or simply promote meetings of groups with common interests, ideas, or needs. There are special interest groups on most campuses for virtually anything you may possibly be interested in. And, if you can't find what you're looking for … start something new!

Faculty or Student Associations

These are a form of special interest group in that they are groups of students who belong to the same faculty or area of study who meet on a regular basis. These organizations can be extremely beneficial to you as a student. How? You will regularly be in contact with people studying the same thing you are. They may be in some of your classes or may have already taken some of the classes you are involved in. Your discussions with them will help you stay tuned in to not only what is happening in school, but also in the field you are studying.

These are also excellent groups to become involved with from a networking perspective. There will be students who graduate before you who may be able to assist you in your inevitable career search, and often faculty organizations keep in contact with alumni of the program just for the purpose of keeping abreast of the industry and how it is evolving in the business world.

 Look in your local phone directory for an idea of the special interest groups out there. This will give you some indication of the types of organizations in your area and what you may want to become involved with.

These groups are usually volunteer organizations but offer a wealth of experience for those who get involved. Not only are you meeting and working with people with similar interests, you are involved in the workings of what may be a fairly large and intricately organized group. There may be presidents, chair persons, electorates, committees, and subcommittees.

Don't despair, it's not all strictly business—it may also be a bunch of people hanging out playing poker or talking about the latest interactive CD-ROM! Whatever you're looking for, you will probably be able to find at least two other people on campus that are interested as well. Get together once in a while. You never know what you'll learn!

Some colleges or faculties offer assistance finding work for students that is related to their field of study. Ask your counselor or advisor what job assistance is available to you.

School or Campus Newspapers

Whether it is an official newspaper, or simply a campus bulletin, most schools have some sort of regular publication put together by the student body. This is an excellent learning foundation for people interested in a variety of career paths. From writers and editors, to reporters and typesetters to sales people and advertising trainees, to special interest columnists and editorial writers, a newspaper of any sort is a complex production requiring the cooperation of many professional-minded students who want to gain valuable experience.

Every single one of these is a job jump-start. Get involved with any of them and start building your résumé.

School Sports Teams

Your school sports teams, although a special interest group to a certain degree, are a class unto themselves. Getting involved as an athlete is, of course, an amazing opportunity if you have the skill. If not, there are certainly other ways you can become involved. The difference between a school team and other special interest groups is that the team is run, fundamentally, by the school administration, not by students interested in the team. What this means to you is that you can become involved more as a casual volunteer and not be concerned with the political or bureaucratic end of things.

 A grant is a gift of money to a student that does not need to be repaid. The criteria for grants may vary, but often a certain grade point average is required.

Sports teams need everything from people to help raise funds for equipment or new facilities, to people to sell tickets, to individuals willing to house athletes from other schools in town for competition or tournaments. Again, the benefit to you is meeting like-minded people and learning the ins and outs of coordinating, participating in, and maintaining any organization.

 "Everyone must row with the oars he has."

—English proverb

Business Cooperator Programs

A business cooperator program is an excellent opportunity for students to gain practical experience in the workplace. Local business, large corporations, and sometimes even multinational companies join forces with colleges and universities to provide students with an excellent opportunity to expand their experience beyond classroom learning. The companies offer students part-time, holiday, and/or summer break employment in a variety of positions. This is an amazing opportunity for students to gain practical experience for their résumé. It provides the perfect environment to start networking and building your list of contacts for after graduation.

Sometimes there is a specific student run organization on campus that coordinates this kind of program independently from any faculty. Ask around, because you don't want to miss out on this kind of opportunity.

What's in it for the Company?

First off, they get to scout new talent for their organization and if they find someone they like and feel would fit in, they can begin the training or grooming period early on. Overall these are excellent programs for both students and the business community. Be sure to investigate and find out if your faculty has some kind of arrangement with the business community.

"The difference between what we do and what we are capable of doing would suffice to solve most the world's problems."

—Gandhi

International University Cooperator Programs

These programs are different from the business-based ones, in that they are not necessarily work-related. The university cooperator programs offer students the opportunity to study abroad for up to a year of their total education. Granted, this is not direct work experience but the benefits are certainly still there. You are exposed to a different language, culture, and business practice.

As business of all kinds becomes more global, people with travel experience, knowledge of another language, and a willingness to experience other countries will find themselves at a distinct advantage over other job applicants who are unable or unwilling to enter the global workplace.

 "It is well to remember that the entire population of the universe, with one trifling exception, is composed of others."

—John Andrew Holmes

Remember, employers are looking for employees who are well-rounded individuals as well as being educated in their field. Travel of any kind is a great way to round out your education.

What's the Point?

So why bother getting involved in these extracurricular activities when it's all you can do to keep up with the required reading for your classes?

There are a number of reasons.

There is definitely something to be said for involving yourself with a group of people experiencing the same things you are. There is nothing worse than feeling like you're behind in your reading, you have two papers due in ten days, one of which you haven't even started, you don't understand the latest chapter in your physics class, and none of your friends from high school are in college, so they just don't get it. Just to have someone around who is experiencing the same stress you are is a comforting feeling. Having someone you can vent your frustrations with may be the best investment you make in college!

Plus, it's always the second year of your higher education when you find out all the things you did the hard way in your first year!

You've already gone through the agony of:

- adjusting to college life

- adapting to the size of your classes

- no one knowing your name

- the enormous work load

- being constantly behind

- every prof telling you their class is the one that must have priority

And barely survived! And *then* you learn the secrets locked within the student lounge walls!

You find out about:

- the condensed version textbook you could have used

- the exam registry where you can look at exams from previous classes

- the "fast" way to transfer courses

- the coolest little coffee shop around the corner from the engineering building

Now if only you had belonged to some kind of group on campus where there were second and third year students who could have made your initiation into campus life so much less traumatic! Ah well, live and learn ... the hard way! Well, it really isn't that bad. You still have a few more years of study left, and you no doubt have a few things you could still learn from those who have gone before you, so get involved.

 "The things taught in schools are not an education but the means of an education."

—Ralph Waldo Emerson

Now, aside from all the psychological and anti-stress reasons, are the practical, "how do I make myself employable" reasons. Just because you have a degree or a college diploma doesn't mean the doors of the business world will fly open to greet you when you graduate. Things are very competitive, more people are college or university graduates, and it really *does* matter who you know. So, if you can get out there and combine some practical experience with your classroom study and make a few contacts along the way, you'll find yourself ahead of the game after graduation.

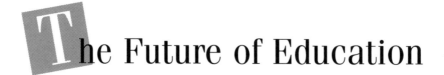

The Future of Education

Although the wheels of change grind slow for large institutions like colleges and universities, the wheels *do* still grind. As the face of business and the technology that accompanies business evolves and progresses, so too must educational institutions, in order to effectively prepare students for the work world.

"Change is not made without inconvenience, even from worse to better."

—Richard Hooker

Indeed, technology is catching up to the school system and it will affect you as a student whether you are prepared for it or not.

How?

Some schools and definitely some faculties are advancing more quickly than others, but all schools are coming into the computer age. As a student, it will affect everything from the way you apply, to the way you hand in assignments, and to the way you communicate with other students and the professor.

Computers and the Application Process

Already some faculties are abandoning the standard paper application form or booklet in favor of a standardized computer disk. When you want to apply to a particular school or faculty you will simply be handed a diskette to return when complete. The disk contains all the information the university needs from you and when it is complete, they simply download the computerized form into their student data base.

This is still a relatively new practice, but don't be surprised to see it take off at most schools.

The computer takes over and you are then processed according to whatever requirements the university deems essential. The computer can categorize according to grade point average, age, program requested, TOEFL scores, education history—*whatever* the faculty wishes—and give them detailed records of applicants. This process has the capability to eliminate a huge amount of paper work and time-consuming organization and filing. Granted, this new system makes a lot of sense, but what if you don't have a computer at home?

Computers are coming down in cost, and if at all possible, it would serve you well to save the money in your piggybank to invest in even a basic computer.

That is the question. Unfortunately these new systems are based on the assumption that *all* students have computers. As we all know, most students would love to have a computer at home and would benefit greatly from it, but not everyone going to school can afford the latest in computer technology.

On the positive side, there are places in all cities, and many smaller towns, that have computers to rent for a nominal fee if you have no other access to a computer. Often libraries have computer centers where people may use their equipment for free, or the university you wish to apply to may offer computer time to those with no convenient access to a computer.

If you have no computer experience whatsoever get some! Take a class at a university or get a friend to show you the ropes on their computer. You must become computer literate—there is no way around it!

College and the Internet

The Internet is something that has been around for quite a number of years and believe it or not, the universities have been on the Internet virtually since its conception. Shortly after the second world war, university laboratories began using computers to send messages, or e-mail, between departments. Electronic mail has been around ever since. Now, of course, with the popularity of the World Wide Web and its graphic qualities, the Internet has become considerably easier to use and to access.

So, what's the point?

Well, with it now being easier to access and to retrieve information off the Net, more and more people are using it as a source for reference material. Also, since most universities have been using e-mail for 40 years, they are naturally going to continue to expand their technology.

Not only is the Internet extremely valuable as an information source, it is also creating a wave of business opportunities. If you know nothing about it ... find out!

What does this mean to you as a student?

Already you can access information about many universities and colleges via the Net and those that do not have Web sites will, no doubt, soon have them. If you are interested in a particular school or program you can send off an e-mail request and the university will send out whatever you request either by mail, or if it is a question that can be addressed with e-mail, that's how you may get your answer.

Additionally, the Internet is a great way to do a little career research. You can put whatever questions you have—be they education- or work-related—out into "computer land" and receive a wealth of information back from people around the world who are on-line. They may be students or people working in the field that interests you. Either way, the information they offer is valuable to you!

At this point you cannot fill out an application for a particular school via the Net, but as the technology continues to improve, that may be the next step.

Unfortunately, once again, the assumption has been made that everyone has, or will have, a computer. If you can't afford one, shop around to find out where you can have access to a computer with Internet capabilities for a reasonable rate. Already Internet cafes offering Internet access (and cappuccino, no doubt) are popping up all over cities and towns. At the very least, you can do a little surfing and find out which schools offer information on-line.

ood for Thought

Whether we are comfortable with it or not, technology and the advance of the computer age is affecting everything we do, including our education and career choices.

How?

Education On-line

We already have computer-assisted learning in many technical schools and computer science programs, so it makes sense for computer learning to take the step to the Internet.

The Internet offers something called "chat rooms." These can be thought of simply as rooms where a group of people with the same interests get together to discuss various topics. There are chat rooms for virtually every topic you can think of—from controversial topics to discussions about your favorite television series. The amazing part about these discussions is they happen in real time. This means there is virtually no delay in time from when I type something in and you are able to read it as it's typed and answer back. Amazing!

 For a list of definitions, please refer to "Terminology Translations" at the end of this book.

So What?

Well, the implications this has for education are enormous. Already we have after-school programs on the Internet for young children who are having difficulty with certain subjects in school. The kids can go on-line from school or from their home, and get help with their homework from a qualified person working on-line at their computer in their own home or office. The kid's questions are answered while they're doing their homework in the comfort of their own home.

Does this mean classrooms will be replaced by computerized chat rooms?

Not likely. A considerable amount of the learning that takes place in universities and colleges is not in the classroom. It takes place in debate groups, over coffee in a student lounge, and in all the other locations where students and professors meet. There is too much to be learned from interacting in person with those who may or may not share your views. That is something the Internet cannot compete with.

 Know that the Internet is a huge information source, one that should be used as a tool—*not* something that replaces getting out and meeting people.

Multimedia Meets the School System

Once again, technology has the potential to change the face of education and the application procedure. Multimedia simply put means the joining of various forms of technology (computers, video images, stereo audio, etc.) to create one complete experience.

As with the Internet, multimedia is bringing with it new opportunities for business and employment. If you are at all interested in a career in technology and its role in business, take a look at both of these explosive fields.

So how does this all affect you as a student applying for college or university?

With the improving multimedia technology linking stereo, video, and computers, college programs where you once had to audition or attend a personal interview may revise their application procedures.

How?

The technology already exists for video conferencing, and as that technology improves, you may find yourself at home in California auditioning in front of a computer and video camera, not a panel of auditors in New York. The same possibilities exist for personal interviews for entrance into specific colleges or faculties.

As education enters the computer age we will, no doubt, see alternatives to today's institutional learning. Education that was once necessarily located in the classroom with an instructor may soon be customized with a computer, fax modem, and interactive CD-ROM.

"Thinking is like loving and dying—each of us must do it for ourself."

—Josiah Royce

After loading your CD, an instructor would guide you through the learning process at a rate that is comfortable or challenging enough for you. Think of this as the computer meeting learning by correspondence. Instead of mailing papers and assignments, you would e-mail them to an instructor who would then grade them and e-mail them back.

Certainly the technology exists for this type of thing to occur, but whether students will see the demise of the campus existence remains to be seen.

Change is inevitable, even if it comes slow. Do make an effort to stay somewhat current with advances in technology. This is the computer era and there is simply no way around having it affect your life. Advances in technology are creeping into the education system and you will be expected to adapt. You might as well prepare yourself as best you can! Technological advances are fascinating … accept them, and enjoy the journey!

Remember, technology is for your use and for your benefit. Don't become so consumed or overwhelmed by it that you forget its function.

Conclusion

Once you're accepted into college, your work is done! Well, maybe not all of it, you still have to graduate. Commit to doing your best in college just like you were committed to getting in and you will succeed—maybe even at the top of your class!

"The greatest use of life is to spend it for something that will outlast it."

—William James